OCEANS
& SEAS

Margaret Hynes

KINGFISHER

NEW YORK

KINGFISHER
LONDON & NEW YORK

Copyright © Kingfisher 2010
Published in the United States by Kingfisher,
175 Fifth Ave., New York, NY 10010
Kingfisher is an imprint of Macmillan Children's Books, London.
All rights reserved.

Consultant: David Burnie

Illustrations by Thomas Bayley
Peter Bull Art Studio
Mick Posen/www.the-art-agency.co.uk

Distributed in the U.S. by Macmillan, 175 Fifth Ave., New York, NY 10010
Distributed in Canada by H.B. Fenn and Company Ltd., 34 Nixon Road, Bolton, Ontario L7E 1W2

Library of Congress Cataloging-in-Publication data has been applied for.

ISBN: 978-0-7534-6541-7

Kingfisher books are available for special promotions and premiums. For details contact:
Special Markets Department, Macmillan, 175 Fifth Ave., New York, NY 10010.

For more information, please visit www.kingfisherbooks.com

Printed in China
1 3 5 7 9 8 6 4 2
1SCHOL/0510/WKT/UNT/140MA/C

Note to readers: The website addresses listed in this book are correct at the time of publishing.
However, due to the ever-changing nature of the Internet, website addresses and content can change.
Websites can contain links that are unsuitable for children. The publisher cannot be held responsible for
changes in website addresses or content, or for information obtained through third-party websites.
We strongly advise that Internet searches be supervised by an adult.

The Publisher would like to thank the following for permission to reproduce their material. Every care has been taken to trace copyright holders. However, if there have been unintentional omissions or failure to trace copyright holders, we apologize and will, if informed, endeavor to make corrections in any future edition (t = top, b = bottom, c = center, r = right, l = left):

Front cover (turtle) Frank Lane Picture Agency (FLPA)/Reinhard Dirscherl; front cover (diver) Shutterstock/Jim Lopes; front cover (anemone) Shutterstock/Sergey Galushko; front cover (puffin) Shutterstock/Chris Alcock; front cover (dolphin) Getty/Frederic Pacorel; front cover (angelfish) Shutterstock/D. J. Mattaar; front cover (jellyfish) Shutterstock/Geanina Bechea; 4tl Photolibrary/Paul Kay; 4bl NaturePL/Jurgen Freund; 4–5b Photolibrary/Stephen Frink; 4br FLPA/Reinhard Dirscherl; 5cl NaturePL/Jose B. Ruiz; 5tr FLPA/Reinhard Dirscherl; 5r Natural History Picture Agency (NHPA)/Michael Patrick O'Neill; 5cr Seapics/Ross Armstrong; 5bl Seapics/Ross Armstrong; 5b Seapics/Ross Armstrong; 6tl Photolibrary/Allan White; 6bl Photolibrary/Tim White; 6cr Photolibrary/Charles Marden Fitch; 6br Corbis/Theo Allofs; 7c Science Photo Library (SPL)/Martin Jakobsson; 7cr Corbis/NASA; 7bc Photolibrary/Allan White; 8tr Alamy/Idris Ahmed; 9bl SPL/Eye of Science; 11c Neptune Project, University of Washington; 11br SPL/Dr. Ken Macdonald; 12–13ct Corbis/Nic Bothma; 12–13c Corbis/Nic Bothma; 13bl Corbis/Dadang Tri/Reuters; 13tr Shutterstock/A. S. Zain; 13br Getty/Philippe Huguen/AFP; 14bl Photolibrary/Tony Waltham; 14tr Alamy/eye35.com; 14cr Corbis/moodboard; 14br Getty/Martin D. Reynolds/Flickr; 15 NaturePL/Jouan Ruis; 15tc NaturePL/Chris Gomershall; 15b NaturePL/David Tipling; 16b Photoshot/AllCanada Photos; 17b Photolibrary/Richard Herrmann; 18b NASA; 19tl NHPA/Bill Coster; 20tl Shutterstock/Wolfgang Amri; 20bl Shutterstock/Luis Chavier; 20c Shutterstock/ivvv1975; 20cr Shutterstock/Olga Khoroshunova; 20br Shutterstock/Rui Gomes; 20–21 Shutterstock/John A. Anderson; 21cl Alamy/David Fleetham; 21cr Shutterstock/Milena Katzer; 21b Shutterstock/Rich Carey; 22c SPL/M. I. Walker; 22–23 Shutterstock/Peter J Kovacs; 23cr NaturePL/David Shale; 25tr Photolibrary/moodboard; 25bl NaturePL/Dan Burton; 25br Image Quest Marine/Peter Batson; 26tr Shutterstock/nice_pictures; 26cr Alamy/WILDLIFE GmbH; 26cl Alamy/WILDLIFE GmbH; 26bl Photolibrary/James Watt; 27t Seapics/Rowan Byrne; 27bl Alamy/Mark Conlin; 27br Corbis/Frans Lanting; 28br Alamy/David Fleetham; 28tl Seapics/Robert L. Pitman; 30c The Art Archive/Harper Collins; 30bl Alamy/North Wind Pictures; 31cl The Art Archive/Private Collection; 31cr Bridgeman Art Library/Worshipful Company of Clockmakers' Collection; 32–33 Getty/National Geographic Society; 32b Shutterstock/Rich Carey; 33bl SPL/Alexis Rosenfeld; 33br Consortium for Ocean Leadership; 34bl Getty/Terence Spencer/Time & Life Pictures; 34bc Franck Goddio/Hilti Foundation/Christoph Gerigk; 34br Franck Goddio/Hilti Foundation/Christoph Gerigk; 34–35 Alamy/Poelzer; 35c Corbis/Ralph White; 35br Shutterstock/Sergey Popov; 36cl Mike Page/National Institute of Water & Atmospheric Research, New Zealand; 36b Photolibrary/Hein Van Den Heuvel; 36–37 Photolibrary/Upperhall Upperhall; 37tr Photolibrary/Tobias Bernhard; 37b Photolibrary/Greig Cranna; 38tr SPL/Martin Bond; 38bl Rob McKoen; 40tr Alamy/Interfoto; 40b Corbis/Martin Harvey; 40–41 Shutterstock/Photofish; 41tr Alamy/Images & Stories; 41c Corbis/Akhtar Soomro/epa; 41bl Corbis/Academy of Natural Sciences, Philadelphia; 41br Press Association/AP; 42tr Alamy/Don Tonge; 42bl Alamy/Eric Nathan; 42–43 Photolibrary/Splashdown Direct; 43t Corbis for Action Aid/Gideon Mendel; 48tr Press Association/AP; 48cl Alamy/Francisco Martinez; 48br NaturePL/Adam Burton; 48bl Photolibrary/Peter Bennett.

CONTENTS

LIFE IN THE OCEANS

From the seashore to the deepest depths, oceans are home to the most diverse life on Earth. Plants are found only in the sunlit parts of the ocean. Animals are found at all depths, though more than 90 percent of all marine species dwell on the seabed, where a single rock can be home to as many as ten major groups of animals, such as corals, mollusks, and sponges.

Mammals

All mammals need air to breathe, so you might be surprised to find mammals living in the sea. There are many sea mammals, however, including dolphins, such as this one (right), sea lions, walrus, whales, porpoise, and manatees. They all come up to the surface to breathe air, and like land mammals, they give birth to live young.

Fish

Fish are the most diverse group of animals in the oceans. There are more than 15,300 known species of marine fish, and scientists believe that there are thousands more to be discovered. New fish species are being logged at an average rate of three per week.

Echinoderms

Starfish, sea urchins, and sea cucumbers are all echinoderms. This group of spiny-skinned animals, found only in the oceans, contains about 6,000 species. Echinoderms are simple animals, lacking a brain and complex sensing organs.

> Oceans contain 99 percent of all living space on the planet.

Plantlike animals

Anemones, sponges, and sea squirts are marine animals, but they look and behave more like plants. Instead of searching for their food, they stay fixed in one spot and wait for floating planktonic creatures to come into their reach.

Ocean forests

Forests of giant seaweeds called kelp provide a home and hunting ground for many different creatures in the shallow, cool waters above rocky seabeds. The towering kelp hold on to the rocky bottom with rootlike structures called holdfasts.

Crustaceans

Crabs and other types of crustaceans, including shrimp, lobsters, and barnacles, have hard skeletons on the outside of their bodies. Crabs and shrimp can swim, but lobsters can only scuttle along the seabed. Barnacles stick to a hard spot and never move.

WATERY PLANET

Most of us probably think of our world as being solid ground, but about 70 percent of the planet's surface is actually covered by salt water. The largest areas of this water, between the continents, are called oceans. Areas of salt water that are closer to the land, or partly or completely surrounded by land, are called seas.

World ocean

There are five oceans: the Pacific Ocean, Atlantic Ocean, Indian Ocean, Southern Ocean, and Arctic Ocean. Channels of water link these oceans to form one gigantic body of water. The Pacific Ocean is larger than the other four oceans put together, reaching halfway around the world.

WATER CYCLE

The oceans exchange water with the atmosphere in a never-ending cycle. Heat from the Sun turns water at the ocean's surface into water vapor. This rises into the sky, where it then cools and turns back to droplets of water that form clouds. The clouds spill rain and snow, which form streams, rivers, and glaciers that flow back to the ocean. Even the water that seeps into the ground finds its way back to the ocean.

water freezes and falls as snow

wind blows clouds inland

water vapor rises from the ocean

plants lose water to the air

rain falls on the ocean

water vapor rises from lakes

rivers and streams flow into the ocean

Rain washes salt out of the rocks and into rivers, which carry it to the ocean. This makes the ocean salty.

Ocean trade link

Every year, about 50,000 ships carrying one-fourth of the world's freight use the Strait of Malacca as a shortcut between the Pacific and Indian oceans. The channel is one of the busiest shipping routes in the world.

Sea feature

About 115,830 sq. mi. (300,000km²) of seabed below the warm, shallow waters of the tropics are covered in hedgelike structures called coral reefs. The Great Barrier Reef off the coast of Australia, in the Pacific Ocean, is the world's largest coral reef system.

"How inappropriate to call this planet Earth when it is quite clearly ocean."

Arthur C. Clarke (1917–2008)
Science-fiction author, inventor, and futurist

Ocean storm

Hurricanes are one of the most destructive forces created by oceans. They form in tropical regions out at sea, where cold winds meet warm winds. The air begins to swirl, and a spinning column of storm clouds builds up. The strong winds and heavy rain cause havoc when they reach land.

Fresh water in the sea

Although icebergs are found floating in the salty ocean, they are actually made of fresh water. The dissolved salts in seawater make it denser than fresh water, which is one of the reasons why icebergs can float. Icebergs break off glaciers and ice shelves at the frozen poles.

ANCIENT OCEANS

The first ocean on Earth was formed very early in the planet's 4.6-billion-year history. The oldest known rocks, which have features showing they originally formed on an ocean floor, are dated to about 4 billion years ago. This means that one global ocean probably existed before the continents. It was split up by continents forming from volcanic eruptions and slowly drifting across the face of the planet on moving plates of Earth's crust.

Gases and water vapor from inside Earth erupt from the volcano.

Single-celled algae were floating in the sunlit areas of the oceans from about 2 billion years ago.

Earliest ocean

Most of the water on Earth was probably released as water vapor by volcanoes and vents roughly 4.2 billion years ago. Eventually, the vapor cooled into rain that poured down to create a global ocean. Fossils of sea-dwelling cyanobacteria show that there was life in the ocean at least 3.5 billion years ago. We know that cyanobacteria formed stony structures, called stromatolites, because the bacteria still form these structures today.

> The Atlantic Ocean is getting wider by 1 in. (25mm) per year.

Meteorite brings water in the form of vapor to the planet.

High and dry

The really interesting thing about this fossil of a sea-dwelling ammonite is that it was found in rocks high up in the Himalayas in Asia. This proves that the mountains were once part of the sea floor. They formed when India drifted north and crashed into Asia, pushing seabed rocks 5 mi. (8km) into the air.

Rivers of lava contain water vapor from deep inside Earth.

http://marinebio.org/Oceans/History

Vents in the seabed spit out boiling-hot water.

Mats of cyanobacteria build in layers to form a stromatolite.

⊖ DRIFTING APART

240 million years ago

One giant ocean, Panthalassa, surrounded the supercontinent of Pangaea 290–240 million years ago (m.y.a.). After this period, Pangaea broke up, with part drifting north and part drifting south. The northern part split to form the North Atlantic Ocean 208–146 m.y.a. From 146 m.y.a., the South Atlantic and Indian oceans began to form. The oceans are still changing shape today.

208 million years ago

146 million years ago

today

SUBDUCTION ZONE—an area where one tectonic plate is diving beneath another into the interior of Earth

UNDER THE SEA

Just a century ago, very little was known about the ocean floor. Following the invention of sonar and echo-sounding equipment in the 1920s and deep-sea diving craft in the 1930s, we now know that the ocean floor is a world of vast plains, huge mountains, active volcanoes, and deep chasms called trenches. Many of these are formed by the movement of the tectonic plates that make up Earth's crust.

An island is formed when the summit of a volcano rises above the surface of the water.

A volcanic island arc forms where tectonic plates meet.

Deep trenches occur where two plates push against each other and one slides under the other.

A seamount is an extinct volcano that does not rise above the surface of the water.

Ocean floor

Much of the ocean floor is a flat plain, covered with a deep layer of fine particles, called ooze. Chains of underwater mountains run the length of all the oceans. Along each ridge, lava bubbles up and cools to form new sea floor as plates move away on either side. Trenches descend in subduction zones where plates collide. Here, volcanoes have burst up to create seamounts. Some of the volcanoes reach the ocean surface as volcanic islands.

Hot, soft mantle moves slowly like a conveyor belt, carrying plates of crust.

> Standing at 33,474 ft. (10,203m), Mauna Kea, Hawaii, is the tallest mountain, but most of it lies under the ocean.

Continental slope

At the edges of the continents, the sea is relatively shallow and is a hunting ground for sea birds. But usually within a few miles of land the seabed starts to slope downward into the black depths.

A mid-ocean ridge is formed where plates pull apart and magma rises up to fill the gaps, creating new ocean floor.

www.indiana.edu/~gl05lab/1425chap13.htm

Hydrothermal vents

Dark plumes of hot, mineral-rich water gush out of hydrothermal vents in Earth's crust. Over time, the minerals settle around the vents to form chimneys.

Deep dive

In 1960, the U.S. Navy sent the *Trieste* submersible down into the Marianas Trench in the Pacific Ocean. It took almost five hours to complete the descent to the bottom, which was almost 7 mi. (11km) down.

⊖ SONAR

Scientists onboard ships use sonar to map the ocean floor. The scientists direct sound waves at the bottom and chart the echoes that bounce back to create images, such as this one of an area of the Pacific's mid-ocean ridge. Different colors show different depths. Dark blue is the deepest; red is the shallowest.

map created from sonar data

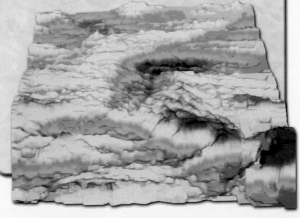

WAVES

Ocean waves are ripples of energy. Most waves are caused by winds as they brush against the top of the ocean and transfer energy from the air to the water. While the wave energy moves forward through the ocean, pushed in the direction of the wind, the water does not move any great distance.

> EPICENTER—the point on Earth's surface directly above the focus of an earthquake

Direction of wave movement

The crest is the high point of the wave.

The crest topples forward and breaks on the beach.

The trough is the low point of the wave.

The wave gets higher as the seabed rises.

The water in each wave moves in circles.

Making waves

Each wave of energy lifts water particles around in circles, creating visible crests and troughs on the surface. As waves approach a shore, the circulation of water at the bottom of the wave is slowed down by the seabed and the top spills over.

Surf's up!

The farther waves travel while still being blown by the wind, the bigger they get. This means that persistent winds over great wide oceans uninterrupted by land, such as the Pacific, generate huge waves. Surfers flock to beaches where such waves break on land because these beaches provide the best and most consistent wave-riding conditions.

> Greek historian Thucydides put forward the theory that underwater earthquakes cause tsunamis in 426 B.C.

⊖ TSUNAMIS

Sometimes reaching heights of 130 ft. (40m) or more, tsunamis are incredibly destructive waves. They are triggered by submarine earthquakes, volcanoes, or landslides. The larger the disturbance, the larger and more dangerous the tsunami.

water is suddenly elevated

low-lying land is in danger of being submerged

direction of movement of continental plate

earthquake epicenter

oceanic plate is submerged below continental plate

Scientists have designed a network of sensors, floating receivers, and satellites to detect and monitor tsunamis while they are still far out at sea. This early warning system could give people time to save themselves.

The information that this buoy receives from a sensor on the seabed is beamed to a satellite, which then sends it to a warning station on land.

Tsunami destruction

In 2004, the Asian tsunami flattened coastal settlements in Indonesia, Sri Lanka, and India. About 230,000 people lost their lives and hundreds of thousands of people were left homeless.

Storm waves

On calm days waves barely move, but in storms they move faster and faster and grow higher and higher. These storm waves often cause havoc if they reach land, particularly if they break in built-up areas where the sea defenses are designed to handle only much smaller waves.

COASTS

A coast is the edge of the land where it meets the sea or ocean. The variety and types of plants and animals living on a stretch of coastline depends on the type of coast that it is. Sandy beaches, towering cliffs, and sheltered harbors are all types of coasts. The shape of the coastline is always changing. Over time, some coasts are worn away by waves, while other coasts are built up by sand and pebbles washed ashore.

Hard rock withstands the powerful force, but soft rock soon crumbles.

▼ HEADLAND—an area of land protruding out to sea

Beach protection

Beaches absorb wave energy, which means they are a coast's best form of defense against the sea. However, when waves strike a beach, they wash sand or pebbles across the beach at an angle. Fences called groins can help keep beaches in place.

Shaping coasts

Waves wear away rocks by pounding them with water and hurling stones at them. On some coasts, waves scoop out hollows in the sides of headlands to form caves. Eventually, these turn into arches that go right through the headland. If the arch roof collapses, a free-standing stack is formed.

⊖ DANGEROUS COASTS

At night and in fog, lighthouses shine bright beams out to sea, warning sailors that they are dangerously close to land. Even in good visibility, many coasts hold dangers for sailing vessels. Jagged rocks under the water can damage and sink a boat, or the boat could hit a hidden sandbank. Some coasts are well known for rough seas that can force a boat onto the rocks or to run aground in shallow waters.

Giant waves threaten a lighthouse.

> The coastlines of the world measure 1 million mi. (1.6 million km) in total.

A puffin can dive
82 ft. (25m) into
the water.

Life on the cliffs

Cliffs may look bare, but you can find wildlife on
all levels of these rocky façades. Rabbits, foxes, and
insects are found among the plants on the flat tops
of cliffs. Here, if the soil is deep enough, puffins dig
burrows to lay their eggs in or move in to old rabbit
holes. Other birds, such as razorbills and guillemots,
prefer to lay their eggs on ledges in the cliff face,
where nonflying predators cannot reach them.

OCEANS IN MOTION

CURRENT—*a flow of water in a definite direction*

Ocean water is always on the move. The Moon's gravity pulls ocean water toward it as it orbits Earth, so a bulge of ocean water follows the Moon around. Another bulge forms on the opposite side of the world. The result is the rise and fall of coastal water levels, called tides. Surface water swirls around the globe in powerful currents, taking the weather with it. Currents also flow vertically in the ocean.

KEY

1. Shore crab
2. Mussels
3. Barnacles
4. Hermit crab
5. Common starfish
6. Sea anemone
7. Prickleback (a fish)

High or dry

Twice a day, the ocean comes high up on the beach and then goes back again. In some places, the difference is extreme, with the deep water at high tide allowing sailboats in and out of the harbor. But at low tide, the water is so shallow that boats either become stuck or they are isolated at sea, unable to reach the harbor.

Rockpool ecosystem

When the tide goes out from a rocky coast, hollows in the rocks hold on to pools of water. Each one is a miniature ecosystem. Limpets and periwinkles graze on seaweed. Crabs munch on shellfish, and pricklebacks nibble barnacles and green seaweed. Life in the rock pool is hard. The wildlife must be able to cope with drastic changes in the water, salt, oxygen, and temperature levels in the pool.

> The biggest tidal range is at the Bay of Fundy, Canada. The difference in height between high and low tide is 52 ft. (16m).

http://oceanmotion.org

Warm and cold currents

Surface currents are driven by the wind, so they are closely linked to global wind patterns. These are affected by the heat of the Sun and the rotation of Earth. The currents move clockwise in the north and counter-clockwise in the south, carrying warm water toward the poles and cold water to the tropics.

Gulf stream current

cold current

warm current

Benguela current

Humboldt (Peru) current

● UPWELLING ZONES

Ocean currents can move vertically as well as sideways. Upwelling currents carry nutrients from deep in the ocean up to the sunlit surface. The nutrients provide food for tiny floating animals called zooplankton, which multiply rapidly, creating a plentiful supply of food for fish. The fish form rich fisheries that attract many fishermen.

thousands of tuna at an upwelling zone off Peru

SALT MARSHES AND DELTAS

Some coastal areas, such as river estuaries and sheltered bays, do not experience direct wave action. Instead, the rivers deposit mud particles onto the shore, while the seas deposit silts and sand sediments. These build up to form tidal flats, which are flooded when the tide comes in. Often the flats are colonized by salt-tolerant plants, called halophytes. On cool coasts the plants form grassy or shrubby salt marshes, but in tropical regions trees known as mangroves form dense, tidal swamp forests.

Bird food

Estuary mud flats are a buffet for birds. Worms, crabs, shrimp, and mollusks are all on the menu. Oystercatchers have long beaks to probe deep in the mud for shrimp. Other birds have differently shaped beaks, depending on how they catch their prey.

⊜ DELTA FORMATION

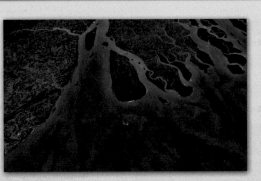

Ganges Delta, Bangladesh

This aerial view of the Ganges River estuary shows how land is formed where the mighty river meets the ocean. The river flows down to the sea under the force of gravity, carrying mud particles with it. These settle onto the seabed when the channel reaches sea level and loses momentum. The mud builds up into banks, which are colonized by plants, forming a delta crossed by many rivers.

Sea grasses are halophytes (salt-tolerant plants).

Manatees graze on sea grasses and mangrove leaves. They eat up to 10 percent of their body weight each day.

> With 3 oz. of sediment per gallon (22,000mg per liter), the Huang He (Yellow River) is the world's muddiest river.

Mangrove swamp

An almost impenetrable tangle of prop roots anchor the mangrove trees, while other roots shoot upward to avoid the salt and help the trees breathe. The swamps are full of birds, insects, fish, crabs, and snails and attract many predators. Mangrove swamps and salt marshes both form buffers that protect the land from flooding and prevent it from being worn away by the sea. The plants adapt to rising sea levels by simply growing farther inland.

www.globio.org/glossopedia/article.aspx?art_id=39

Mudskippers climb up mangrove tree roots as the tide comes in, to avoid predators.

Crocodiles penetrate deep into the forest through twisting mangrove channels.

Hawksbill turtles take refuge from fishermen in mangrove swamps.

CORAL REEFS

"Every one must be struck with astonishment, when he first beholds one of these vast rings of coral-rock, often many leagues in diameter . . ."

Charles Darwin (1809–1882)
The Structure and Distribution of Coral Reefs, 1842

Coral reefs flourish in shallow, clean waters in the tropics. These solid structures are built up from the remains of marine animals called corals. Reefs grow slowly as the animals that form their living surfaces multiply, spread out, and die, adding their skeletons to the reef. Many people rely on reefs as a source of food and tourist income. The reefs also protect coasts from wave erosion. Some islands are made entirely of coral.

Prickly predator

A hungry crown-of-thorns starfish climbs up on coral and pulls its stomach out of its mouth and over its prey. The starfish releases digestive juices that dissolve the coral down to its skeleton, and then the starfish's stomach absorbs nutrients from the liquefied particles.

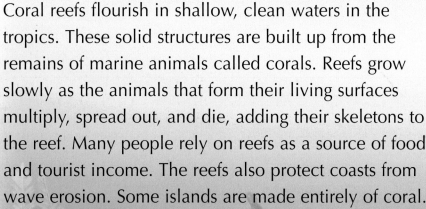

Underwater garden

A healthy reef bursts with life and color, similar to the way a rainforest does on land. Even the smallest reefs are teeming with hundreds of different types of corals, fish, crabs, starfish, sea urchins, and other animals. Sadly, reefs are under threat from human activity. They are broken up for building materials, damaged by divers, and suffer from the poisonous effects of coastal pollution.

∨ ATOLL—*a coral island shaped like a ring, with a lagoon in the middle of it*

> Some coral reefs have been growing for about 50 million years and are over 3,280 ft. (1,000m) thick.

⊖ FORMATION OF A CORAL ATOLL

Coral reefs often fringe volcanic islands where the water is warm, shallow, and light. As the island is worn away by geological processes and begins to sink, more coral grows on top of existing coral to stay in the warmer, lighter surface waters, and a barrier reef builds up. A lagoon, or wide stretch of water, separates the coral reef from the island. The island continues to sink. When it disappears completely, a coral atoll is left behind.

coral encircles island   island is reduced   coral ring remains

http://coris.noaa.gov/about

Danger in the dark

When night falls, whitetip reef sharks emerge from sandy coral caves and burst into frenzied activity, seeking out coral fish hidden deep in the reef. These nocturnal creatures are among the largest predators on reefs.

6

7

KEY

1 Queen angelfish

2 Clownfish

3 Giant sea anemone

4 Crown-of-thorns starfish

5 Yellow cube trunkfish

6 Lionfish

7 Queen angelfish

OCEAN ZONES

Scientists divide the oceans into layers, or zones. Each one is distinguished by the amount of sunlight it receives, the depths it occupies, and the levels of pressure found there. With increasing depth, the light fades, the water gets colder, and the water pressure increases with the added weight of the water above. Obviously, the creatures that live in the sea are not aware of the zones—some animals stay in a single zone all their lives, but others move between different zones.

Plankton float on the surface, where the sunlight is the brightest.

Sunlit zone

This zone stretches from the water's surface to 660 ft. (200m) below sea level. Here there is enough light for aquatic plants and algae to photosynthesize (use sunlight to create food). Plankton drift in the sunlit surface waters, attracting grazers, who in turn attract predators, such as tuna, turtles, and diving birds, including guillemots. More than 90 percent of all marine life exists in this zone.

Twilight zone

Beneath the sunlit zone and down to 3,280 ft. (1,000m) lies the twilight zone. It is too dark for photosynthesis to take place, but there is just enough light to hunt by. The animals in this zone tend to have large eyes to cope with the dim light. Some of them, including the lantern fish and the flashlight fish, move up into the food-rich sunlit zone at night to feed.

⬤ LIGHT FILTER

White sunlight contains all the colors of the spectrum: red, orange, yellow, green, blue, and violet. When sunlight shines into deep water, red and orange are filtered out in the top 50 ft. (15m) of the ocean. Most other colors are absorbed in the next 130 ft. (40m), with the exception of blue, which penetrates down to 1,560 ft. (475m). Many of the animals that live at depths devoid of red light are red in color, to avoid detection by predators.

Royal red shrimp

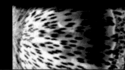

> BIOLUMINESCENT LIGHT—*a light emitted by some animals, using an organ in their bodies called a photophore*

Water conditions

At depths of 660 ft. (200m), there is barely any light and the water pressure is 20 times greater than at the surface. Pressures in the dark zone are more than 100 times greater than at the surface—enough pressure to crush your lungs completely. The water here is bitterly cold, hovering between 36°F (2°C) and 39°F (4°C).

"I have no doubt that from however great a depth we may be able to bring up mud and stones of the bed of the ocean, we shall find them teeming with animal life; the extreme pressure at the greatest depth does not appear to affect these creatures."

Sir James Clark Ross (1800–1862)
In Antarctica, 1841

Dark zone

Beyond 3,280 ft. (1,000m) deep is the dark zone. Food is scarce here, and the animals rely on what little drifts down from above. Most dark-zone fish have gaping mouths to make the best of what food there is. The only light in this zone is bioluminescent light, produced by some of the animals to lure prey or confuse predators.

A sea spider's stiltlike legs help it walk on the oozy ocean floor. This creature lives at depths of up to 24,280 ft. (7,400m).

❯ The deepest-living fish known, *Abyssobrotula galatheae*, was found in the Puerto Rican Trench, 27,467 ft. (8,372m) down.

www.srh.noaa.gov/jetstream/ocean/layers_ocean.htm

The great white shark is the top predator in this food chain.

Common dolphins enjoy a diet of fish, including cod, hake, mackerel, and sardines.

OCEANS IN BALANCE

Plants and animals in the ocean depend on each other. As on land, life in the ocean gets its energy from the Sun. The energy is passed from plant to animal and from animal to animal in the form of food. Marine plants use sunlight to make their own food by changing water and carbon dioxide into sugar and starch through a process called photosynthesis. Animals eat the plants. In return, the animals breathe out carbon dioxide and produce manure that provides nutrients for plants.

Food chain

Seaweeds and grasses grow only in shallow water where there is enough sunlight for them to make their own food. The rest of the ocean's plant life consists of tiny floating plant plankton, called phytoplankton. Most large animals cannot feed on phytoplankton, which is eaten by animal plankton, called zooplankton, instead. Zooplankton are eaten by small fish, which are, in turn, food for larger predators. This is a food chain, part of a more complex food web.

> Great white sharks are the largest predatory fish on Earth. They grow to an average of 15 ft. (4.6m) in length.

*"Third fish: I marvel how the
fishes live in the sea.*

*First fish: Why, as men do a-land;
the great ones eat up the little ones."*

William Shakespeare (1564–1616)
Pericles, Prince of Tyre

Perfect partners

The tips of a giant sea anemone's tentacles
are packed with powerful stinging cells.
Clownfish are immune to the sting and so
live within the tentacles, safe from
predators. In return for the protection it
gets, the clownfish acts as bait, luring
larger fish to the anemone. The clownfish
also cleans the anemone by eating its dead
tentacles and the debris in and around it.

*Krill are a shrimplike
zooplankton.*

*Cod eat many different
types of marine
creatures and are part
of a complex food web.*

*Herring eat
zooplankton.*

*Phytoplankton
include diatoms,
coccolithophores
(shown here), and
cyanobacteria.*

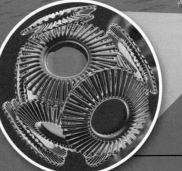

No chain

The basking shark can grow to up to 33 ft. (10m)
long, which makes it the second-largest fish in the
ocean after the whale shark. In spite of its great
size, and unlike most other sharks (which are
predators at the top of the food chain), the basking
shark feeds mainly on plankton. By swimming
with its mouth wide open, it filters plankton out
of the water with its tightly set gill rakers.

⊜ DEEP-SEA COMMUNITY

**giant
tubeworm**

When scientists discovered hydrothermal vents on
the deep ocean floor in 1977, they were surprised
to find an ecosystem of animals living around the
vents. In spite of the boiling water temperatures
and the toxic soup of chemicals produced at the
vent, giant tubeworms, fish, crabs, shrimp, clams,
and anemones were thriving. These animals do
not depend on sunlight for their source of energy.
Instead, they feed on tiny bacteria that get their
energy directly from the chemicals in the water
through a process known as chemosynthesis.

http://oceanlink.island.net/biodiversity/Foodweb/Foodweb.html

MARINE MIGRATIONS

BREEDING GROUND—*a place where animals of the same species reproduce*

Some marine animals make regular journeys from one area to another, often at the same time of year. These journeys are called migrations. The driving force behind any animal migration is the search for food or breeding grounds. Animal migration in the oceans is more complicated than on land because animals can move both horizontally and vertically through the water.

Atlantic salmon

An Atlantic salmon migrates thousands of miles between the ocean, where it spends most of its life, and the stream in which it breeds. Once it reaches fresh water, the salmon finds its particular stream by sniffing out the unique chemical makeup of the water.

Arctic tern

Every year, Arctic terns migrate from their breeding grounds in the Arctic all the way to Antarctic waters and then back again. This round trip of up to 21,750 mi. (35,000km) allows the tern to enjoy the benefits of two summers.

European eel

European eels travel across the Atlantic Ocean to the Sargasso Sea, near Bermuda, to lay their eggs. The enormous effort takes its toll on the eels, which die of exhaustion. The eggs hatch into tiny, leaf-shaped leptocephalus larvae. These drift back to Europe, pushed along by the ocean currents.

Gray whale

Every year, gray whales travel an incredible 6,000 mi. (9,650km) from their rich feeding grounds in the icy waters off Alaska to the safe, warm coastal lagoons of Baja California in Mexico. There, they give birth to their calves, some of which are picked off by killer whales, or orcas, on their way back north.

> Arctic terns live for up to 30 years, which means the bird can travel up to 620,000 mi. (1 million km) in its lifetime.

www.whaleroute.com/migrate

Leatherback turtle

Adult leatherback turtles migrate from their mild, temperate feeding and foraging areas in North America and Europe to tropical breeding grounds in South America and Africa. Large numbers of leatherback turtles are accidentally killed by fishing fleets during their journey.

leatherback
turtle

Navigation

Scientists believe that some marine animals use ocean currents to find their way. Other animals, including the Atlantic salmon, may detect and follow lines of magnetic force in the surface of Earth to navigate. Oceanic birds, turtles, and mammals might also use the Sun, stars, and familiar landmarks as guides.

Tracking turtles

The tracking device being attached to this leatherback turtle will provide valuable insights into the animal's migratory behavior. Such insights will help conservationists discover when and where the turtle needs protection from human threats, such as fishing.

FROZEN SEAS

There are icy oceans in the polar regions at opposite ends of the globe. The Arctic Ocean in the north is almost completely surrounded by the landmasses of North America, Eurasia, and Greenland. In the south, the Southern Ocean surrounds the Antarctic continent and connects the southernmost parts of the Atlantic, Pacific, and Indian oceans. Of the two polar oceans, the Southern Ocean is the coldest, with surface water temperatures ranging between 28°F (−2°C) and 36°F (2°C). It is also richer in animal life.

Seals have a thick layer of fat, called blubber, under their skin to keep them warm.

Emperor of Antarctica

The emperor penguin is the largest of all the penguin species. Like all penguins, it is flightless, with a streamlined body and wings that are adapted for gliding through the water. Emperor penguins can remain submerged for up to 18 minutes, diving to depths of up to 1,755 ft. (535m) to catch fish and krill.

Southern life

While the Arctic Ocean's temperature is influenced by the warming and cooling of the land that rims it, temperatures in the Southern Ocean are influenced by icy gales that blow down from flat highlands on Antarctica. In the winter, pack ice covers more than half of this ocean and air temperatures drop to between −4°F (−20°C) and −22°F (−30°C). Animals such as sponges, anemones, crabs, and starfish thrive on the seabed away from the howling winds. Birds, seals, whales, fish, and squid wait for the summer, when the ice retreats, to hunt for food in the icy water.

Narwhals

Narwhals live only in the Arctic Ocean. The male narwhal is easily identified by its swordlike, spiral-twisted tusk, which pierces through its upper lip and can be up to 10 ft. (3m) long. The function of the tusk is not clear, but it is believed that rival narwhals may use them against each other during the mating season.

> PACK ICE—*a floating jigsaw puzzle of plates of ice that is free to drift*

KILLER WHALES

The killer whale, or orca, is the top marine predator in both the Southern Ocean and the Arctic Ocean. Despite its name, the killer whale is actually the largest member of the dolphin family. As well as fish, squid, and sea birds, killer whales feast on marine mammals such as seals, sea lions, and even whales, using teeth that can be 4 in. (10cm) long. Killer whales may be trying to locate prey above the surface when they "spyhop" by rising up out of the water and hold the position for several minutes. Killer whales are known to grab seals right off the ice or deliberately upend ice floes to tip the seals into the sea.

Killer whales spyhopping

The Antarctic icefish has antifreeze blood that can withstand the freezing temperatures.

The Antarctic anemone uses its long tentacles to catch starfish, sea urchins, and jellyfish much larger than itself.

Red sea stars live only in very cold waters, where they feed on dead fish, sea sponges, and other sea stars.

Borch live under the pack ice. These fish also have antifreeze blood.

Antarctic sea ice covers between 1.5 million (in summer) and 8.5 million (in winter) sq. mi. of ocean.

www.windows.ucar.edu/tour/link=/earth/polar/polar_oceans.html

EARLY SEA EXPLORERS

"... a better ship for such service
I never could wish for."

James Cook (1728–1779)
on HMS Endeavour

From the 1400s to the end of the 1800s, explorers traveled across the globe in fragile wooden ships, mapping the oceans and any coastlines and islands they encountered. Over time, sailors were able to depend on charts made by earlier explorers, using increasingly sophisticated instruments to pinpoint their position at sea.

Captain Cook

James Cook entered the British navy at the lowest rank, an able seaman, in 1755. By 1775, he had been promoted to the rank of captain. Cook mapped more of the planet's surface than any other individual.

Europeans in Hawaii

The first contact Hawaii had with Europe was when Cook visited there in 1778. The islanders killed Cook in 1779. Despite this, Europeans, inspired by accounts of Cook's travels, were soon visiting the islands. This 19th-century picture shows Europeans in Hawaii in the 1870s.

Cook's endeavors

Although the oceans were fairly well mapped by the 1700s, there were still gaps in maps of the south. One of the explorers who set out to fill the gaps was the English navigator James Cook. Cook made three voyages, the first of which was aboard HMS *Endeavour*. By the time of his death in 1779, Cook had discovered and mapped the eastern coast of Australia and most of the major island groups in the Pacific Ocean. He had also circumnavigated the Antarctic and visited the Arctic through the Bering Strait.

 HMS *Endeavour* was originally built to transport coal and timber.

⊖ FINDING THE WAY

On his first voyage, Cook used astronomical tables and a sextant for navigating his way by the Sun and stars. On his second voyage, Cook tested John Harrison's chronometer, a clock that could give accurate times for use in calculating longitude. It proved to be a success, and chronometers continued to be used by navigators well into the 1900s.

sextant

Harrison's H5 chronometer

The sailors mostly ate boiled beef, which they washed down with a mixture of water and rum, called grog.

Cook and his officers plotted their course on charts in the captain's cabin.

The broad, flat hull was ideal for sailing in the shallow waters of the South Pacific.

www.cookmuseumwhitby.co.uk

"Knowledge of the oceans is more than a matter of curiosity. Our very survival may hinge upon it."

President John F. Kennedy (1917–1963)
Message to Congress, 1961

MODERN EXPLORATION

Today's ocean explorers make voyages of discovery deep below the ocean's surface rather than across it. They are equipped with deep-diving craft and suits that can withstand the extraordinary water pressure at great depths, as well as a range of other technologies. Some modern ocean explorers seek out previously undiscovered forms of life. Others investigate the ocean floor itself. Shipwrecks also lure explorers to the seabed.

❯ BATHYSPHERE—*metal sphere lowered from a ship for deep diving*

Unmanned submersible

A long cable connects this Remotely Operated Vehicle (ROV) to the mother ship, from which operators control the craft, using it to explore, film, measure, and collect samples.

> ❯ In 1930, Dr. William Beebe was lowered into the Atlantic in the first deep-sea submersible, called a bathysphere.

Mother ship

While modern ocean exploration is concerned with the deep sea, explorers still need surface vessels to get close to the investigation site. Once at sea, the mother ship bursts into life as a research station with laboratories, control centers, and launch winches for submersibles. It also becomes a home for scientists, engineers, sailors, and support staff such as cooks. Sometimes they spend months at a time at sea.

⊖ CORE DRILL

Some research ships are equipped with huge drills that can bore into the seabed 26,250 ft. (8,000m) below sea level. The drill bit is a hollow steel tube with cutters at the end. As it cuts into the ocean floor, long cylinders of rock called cores are pushed into the tube. Each core consists of layers of rock. Using a variety of techniques and equipment, scientists analyze the cores and fossils within them to learn about the climate and landscape that existed when the rock layers were formed.

Mini submarine

Manned submersibles are like miniature submarines. The people onboard are protected from the deep-ocean pressure inside a strong capsule. Although the crew cannot reach out and take samples, a jointed arm controlled from inside the vessel allows the crew to grip and retrieve items.

drilling rig on a research ship

Newt suit

A deep-sea pressure suit is a little like a personal submarine. The pressure inside the hard shells of such suits is the same as that at the surface. Drager Newt suits like this one have fluid-filled joints that allow the divers about three-fourths of normal mobility. Newt suits can be used at depths of up to 1,200 ft. (365m).

MARINE ARCHAEOLOGY

We can imagine the ocean rotting wood, rusting metal, and wearing away rock, but it can also preserve shipwrecks and artifacts made of these materials by burying them under a protective layer of seabed mud. These wrecks and artifacts are a valuable source of information for marine archaeologists, who make detailed studies of underwater sites, mapping the area and recording each find.

A diver examines amphorae at a Roman shipwreck in the Red Sea.

Wreck preservation

Wooden shipwrecks, found well preserved in the sea, are often best left where they are. If they are recovered, they need to be sprayed regularly with a waxy solution that prevents them from drying out. The British ship *Mary Rose*, which sank in 1545, is preserved in this way in a museum in Portsmouth, England.

Sunken city

Following a tsunami in A.D. 365 and a series of earthquakes between the 300s and 1300s, much of ancient Alexandria in Egypt became submerged, or sank below the city's harbor. Underwater excavations in 1994 and again in 1996 uncovered a wealth of artifacts, including sphinxes, obelisks, statues, columns, and ancient Greek and Roman shipwrecks.

marble head of Roman princess Antonia Minor (right)

This statue of Isis was found reasonably well preserved in 1996.

www.titanicinbelfast.com

Titanic

In 1912, the luxury ocean liner *Titanic* hit an iceberg on its maiden voyage and sank, killing 1,517 people. After many failed attempts to find the wreck, it was located 2.5 mi. (4km) down on the seabed off Canada in 1985 by Dr. Robert Ballard. A French team used a submersible, *Nautile*, to remove items from the wreck in 1987, angering many people who argued that the wreck should be respected as a grave.

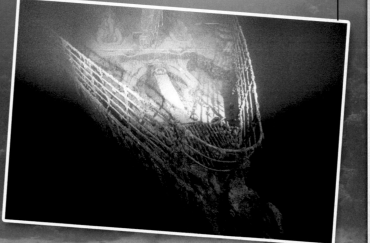

⊜ TREASURE SHIPS

Few shipwrecks contain chests of gold and silver coins, but such treasure wrecks are still to be found. Between the 1500s and 1700s, convoys of Spanish ships carried coins from Latin America to Spain. Many of these ships were hit by storms or sunk in battle and never made it to port.

gold doubloons and silver reales

HARVESTING THE SEA

People extract many different types of animals and plants from the oceans for food, but food is not the only ocean harvest. Pearls are found inside oysters, seaweed is made into fertilizers, fish oils are used to make cosmetics, and medicines come from certain sea creatures. The demand for ocean products is so great that some animals and seaweeds are grown in farms.

∨ FERTILIZER—a natural substance that is added to soil to make it more suitable for growing plants

Useful chemicals

Some sponges produce protective chemicals that prevent other creatures from growing over them. Certain types of these sponges are harvested for their chemicals, which are used to treat illnesses such as malaria and cancer.

Fishy business

Fishing is now a multimillion-dollar global industry, carried out by large boats equipped with electronic fish finders and walls of nets or long lines of hooks. This is so efficient that many fishing grounds are virtually fished out.

Fishing

Fishing has been a way of life for coastal people for thousands of years. Today, most fish are caught at sea by modern fishing vessels using the latest technology. However, some communities still use traditional fishing techniques and catch only what they need, so they never run out of fish. These fishermen in Sri Lanka use rods, watching for fish from their perch on the stilt.

 ＞ *Atlantic Dawn* is the world's largest fishing boat. It is 473 ft. (144.3m) long and has nets the size of two soccer fields.

Pearl farm

In tropical water, pearls may grow around a grain of sand that gets trapped in an oyster's shell. Such pearls are rare and valuable. Most of the pearls sold today are cultivated by pearl farmers, who insert particles into oyster shells and dangle them in the sea until the pearls form.

http://news.bbc.co.uk/cbbcnews/hi/find_out/guides/animals/fishing_and_whaling/

⊖ FISH FARMS

Some kinds of shellfish, and fish such as salmon and trout, are raised in large cages out at sea. The fish are so well fed that they grow much more quickly than they would in the wild. They are also easier to catch because they are trapped in a small area. However, diseases and parasites spread quickly through the tightly packed fish. Any medicine they are given can kill other creatures.

a salmon farm in New Brunswick, Canada

OCEAN ENERGY

About one-third of the world's total reserves of oil and gas lie offshore below the shallow waters. The oceans are also a source of electricity because ocean winds, waves, and tides can all be harnessed to power electricity generators. These power sources could become very important in the future as oil and gas reserves become more difficult to find.

Wave power
One method of generating electricity from wave energy is the Land Installed Marine Power Energy Transmitter (LIMPET). This system creates electricity using turbines powered by the air pressure built up by waves surging in and out of a concrete chamber.

TURBINE—a revolving motor that is pushed around by air, water, or steam

⬤ OIL AND GAS

Pools of oil lie deep inside Earth, trapped by layers of rock. Oil is a fossil fuel, formed from animal and plant life that lived in the seas millions of years ago. When oil is struck offshore, a production platform is installed from which boreholes are drilled to extract the oil. Oil is used as a fuel to make electricity, and it is turned into gasoline. Natural gas collects above oil reserves. It is used as fuel for heating and cooking.

offshore oil platform

 > About 90 million barrels of oil are used in the world every day.

Inside the outer casing, a shaft powers a generator via a gearbox to convert the energy into electricity.

Wind power

Wind turbines use large blades to catch the wind. When the wind blows, the blades rotate, powering a turbine that generates electricity. The stronger the wind, the more electricity is produced. Offshore wind turbines tend to generate more electricity than onshore turbines because ocean winds are usually stronger than those on land, as they meet fewer obstacles.

www.energyquest.ca.gov/story/chapter14.html

Piles driven into the seabed anchor the turbine. The metal above the water is painted a bright color to make it visible to ships. Here, there is an access platform to allow maintenance.

OCEANS IN DANGER

Oceans are so vast that it is difficult to believe that people could do them any harm. But people have harmed the oceans, and they are now in trouble. Overfishing has reduced fish populations in many fishing grounds, while many other species are threatened with extinction because they are trapped and drowned by nets and hooks. The oceans are being poisoned by fertilizers, industrial pollution, sewage, and oil spilled from tankers. Litter has also made its way to the oceans, and coral reefs are being destroyed.

Harmful trade

Traders and hawkers in some tourist centers sell coral, turtle shells, starfish, and dead seahorses. In many parts of the world, the sale of such trinkets is illegal because the trade kills animals and causes damage to their fragile ecosystems. The animals are far more beautiful when they are alive and in their natural environment.

Oily sea birds can be cleaned with water and detergent, but many still die despite this treatment.

Oil spills

Huge quantities of oil are transported at sea by tankers, which can be as long as 1,500 ft. (460m). Sometimes they run aground and spill their oil, causing considerable damage. If sea birds and sea mammals are covered in the oil, they often die from the cold because their clogged feathers or fur no longer contain pockets of air to keep them warm. Animals can also die from consuming the oil as they try to clean themselves.

> Almost 80 percent of the pollutants dumped into the sea come from inland.

Sinking ship

When a tanker runs aground, every effort is made to remove the oil onboard before it spills out. About 35,000 tons of the *Tasman Spirit*'s 74,000-ton cargo was transferred to other vessels before it broke into two, triggering a spill that covered beaches in Karachi, Pakistan, in 2003.

the *Tasman Spirit* sinking in the Arabian Sea off the coast of Pakistan

Under threat

The Mediterranean monk seal is one of the world's most endangered marine mammals. Fewer than 600 survive today. Sometimes they are killed accidentally when they become entangled in fishing nets and drown. Other times they are killed deliberately by fishermen, who consider them pests that steal their fish and damage their nets.

Oil slick

Crude oil is thick, sticky, and poisonous. If it leaks from a tanker, it floats on the surface of the water, forming a slick. This coats everything it touches. Slicks have been known to wash up on beaches hundreds of miles from the spill site.

www.panda.org/about_our_earth/blue_planet/problems/pollution/

EXTINCT SEA BIRD

The great auk bred in colonies on rocky islands and coasts off the North Atlantic. This flightless bird was slaughtered by hunters for food, particularly during the early 1800s. The last breeding pair on Earth was killed in 1844. The great auk's extinction warns us of the consequences of overexploiting marine species.

ICE FLOE—a flat, floating chunk of sea ice that is less than 6 mi. (10km) across its greatest dimension

OCEANS IN THE FUTURE

Over thousands of years, Earth goes through cycles of cooler and warmer global climate conditions. We are in the middle of one of the warm periods, but many scientists believe that modern air pollution is warming up the planet even more than usual through a process called the greenhouse effect. This change in global climate may be affecting the oceans, leading to rises in sea levels and more frequent and more violent ocean storms.

Carbon dioxide

There is 25 percent more carbon dioxide in the atmosphere than there was 150 years ago. The gas is produced by burning fossil fuels in car engines, central heating, and power plants. The extra carbon dioxide in the atmosphere makes the greenhouse effect stronger, possibly causing global warming.

Melting ice

Most of Earth's ice is on land—on Greenland and the continent of Antarctica. Increasing temperatures may be melting the ice more quickly than usual, causing more water to run into the sea, raising sea levels, and causing flooding in low-lying coastal regions. The melting is also destroying polar habitats. Polar bears must now swim longer distances to find food because the ice floes from which they feed are melting, becoming smaller and drifting farther apart.

We can all do our part to help lower greenhouse gases—such as by biking to work or school if possible.

Sea levels have risen by up to 8 in. (20cm) over the past 100 years.

www.atmosphere.mpg.de/enid/1vr.html

Flooding

Scientists predict that Earth's climate will become about 4.5°F (2.5°C) warmer during the 21st century. This heat could make seawater warm up and expand, raising sea levels. The many small islands that lie 3–7 ft. (1–2m) above sea level would disappear and large areas of Bangladesh would be submerged. Floods from storm waves already endanger the lives of many millions of people in Bangladesh.

⊖ GREENHOUSE EFFECT

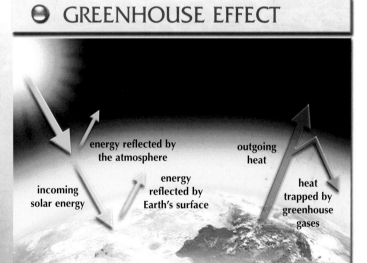

energy reflected by the atmosphere

outgoing heat

incoming solar energy

energy reflected by Earth's surface

heat trapped by greenhouse gases

Greenhouse gases in the atmosphere, including water vapor, carbon dioxide, and methane, cause the greenhouse effect. When sunlight strikes Earth's surface, much of the Sun's energy is absorbed by the planet and then emitted back to space as heat. Greenhouse gases in the atmosphere stop some of this heat from escaping. The more greenhouse gases there are, the more heat is trapped, causing global warming.

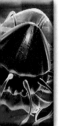

GLOSSARY

algae
Simple, plantlike living things that are able to make their own food using the energy of sunlight.

atmosphere
Layers of gases that surround Earth.

bacteria
Microscopic, single-celled organisms.

carbon dioxide
A colorless gas found in the air. It is one of the greenhouse gases.

climate
The average weather in a region.

community
A collection of organisms living in the same place.

continent
One of seven large sheets of rock that rise above the oceans as dry land.

coral
Hard rock made up of the skeletons of dead animals.

crude oil
Thick, raw oil found inside Earth. It is refined to make petroleum.

delta
A triangular-shaped plain formed from sediments dumped by a river when it meets the sea.

Earth's crust
The rocky outer shell of Earth.

erode
To gradually wear away land by the action of rain, wind, rivers, ice, or the sea.

estuary
A place where fresh water from a river mixes with tidal seawater.

echo-sounding equipment
A machine that measures water depth using sound signals and their echoes.

extinction
When an animal or plant species dies out completely.

global warming
The gradual warming of Earth's climate. It may be caused by pollution in the planet's atmosphere.

gravity
The invisible force of attraction between objects with mass, such as the attraction of Earth and the Moon, which pull toward one another.

habitat
A place where an animal or plant lives and grows.

lava
Hot, melted rock that erupts from volcanoes.

magma
Hot, molten rock that lies below Earth's surface. Once magma reaches the surface, it is called lava.

mantle
The thick layer of hot rock between Earth's crust and core.

methane
A colorless, odorless gas that occurs naturally under the seabed. Also called natural gas, it can be burned as fuel.

migration
A long journey undertaken by animals.

nutrient
A nourishing chemical in food that an organism needs to live and grow.

orbit
To travel in space around a planet or an object. The Moon orbits Earth.

photosynthesis
The chemical process by which plants and algae use sunlight to convert carbon dioxide into food.

phytoplankton
Microscopic floating aquatic plants that make their own food through photosynthesis. Zooplankton and phytoplankton form plankton.

plankton
Living things, often microscopic, that float in ocean water, usually close to the surface.

plate
A giant slab of Earth's crust that moves slowly over the mantle.

polar regions
Areas around the North and South poles.

pollution
The presence in or introduction into the environment of something harmful or poisonous.

predator
An animal that catches and feeds on other animals.

seamount
An underwater mountain formed by a submarine volcano.

sediment
Solid particles, such as sand, mud, or silt, that are transported and deposited by water and wind.

sewage
Human waste and drainage water.

submersible
A small submarine that is designed to explore very deep water.

tide
The rise and fall of the sea level, caused by the gravitational pull of the Sun and the Moon.

tropics
Hot, humid areas north and south of the equator.

twilight zone
The part of the ocean where there is faint blue light. It sits between the sunlit zone and the dark zone.

upwelling
A vertical ocean current.

vent
A hole in the seabed where high-pressure water and minerals are emitted into the ocean.

water pressure
The pressure exerted on part of a column of water. It is caused by the weight of the water above it.

zooplankton
Tiny animals that drift in the water alongside phytoplankton to form plankton.

INDEX

INVESTIGATE

Experience first hand some of the many different aspects of the oceans and seas by visiting seashores, aquariums, and maritime museums, or find out more in books and on websites.

Maritime museums often feature fascinating displays that tell you all about the history of seafaring.

Ocean exploration

Take a trip through time in a maritime museum, where you will find objects and expert information relating to the history of ocean exploration.

The World of Ships by Philip Wilkinson (Kingfisher)

Mystic Seaport: The Museum of America and the Sea, 75 Greenmanville Avenue, Mystic, CT 06355

www.oceanexplorer.noaa.gov

Many modern aquariums have underwater glass walkways that pass through the aquarium itself, allowing you to watch marine animals swimming around you.

Marine animals

Visit an aquarium and experience what life is like underwater. You can also ask experts questions and find out how you can get involved in marine wildlife conservation projects.

Kingfisher Knowledge: Sharks by Miranda Smith (Kingfisher)

John G. Shedd Aquarium, 1200 South Lake Shore Drive, Chicago, IL 60605

http://www.aqua.org   and   www.georgiaaquarium.org

Rock pools are fun to explore, but be careful. Watch where you step, turn over rocks gently, and always leave the pool as you found it.

Beside the seaside

Seashores are wonderful places to discover aquatic plants and animals. Become a wildlife detective and your walk by the sea will become an adventure.

Eyewitness: Seashore by Steve Parker (DK Children)

Monterey, California, and Monterey Bay Aquarium, 886 Cannery Row, Monterey, CA 93940

www.nps.gov/cuis/index.htm

You might like to take part in an organized cleanup, such as this one in Los Angeles, California.

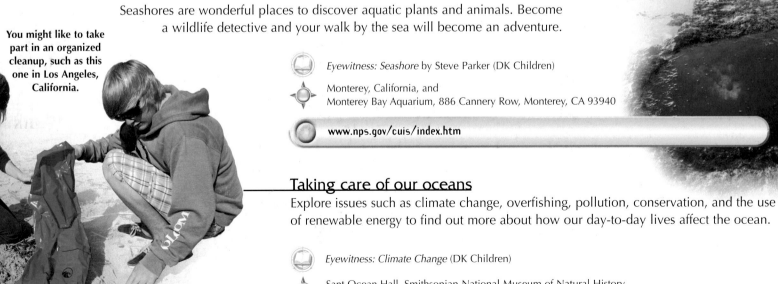

Taking care of our oceans

Explore issues such as climate change, overfishing, pollution, conservation, and the use of renewable energy to find out more about how our day-to-day lives affect the ocean.

Eyewitness: Climate Change (DK Children)

Sant Ocean Hall, Smithsonian National Museum of Natural History, 10th Street and Constitution Avenue, NW, Washington, DC 20560

www.marinebio.com/Oceans/Conservation